THE PYTHON AND ANACONDA

BY
EDITH HOPE FINE

EDITED BY
JUDY LOCKWOOD

PUBLISHED BY
CRESTWOOD HOUSE
NEW YORK

ROCKINGHAM COUNTY PUBLIC LIBRARY

OUTREACH
MADISON
MAYODAN

EDEN
REIDSVILLE
STONEVILLE

J 597.96
F

LIBRARY OF CONGRESS CATALOGING IN PUBLICATION DATA

Fine, Edith Hope.
  The python and anaconda.

  (Wildlife, habits & habitat)
  Includes index.
  SUMMARY: Examines the physical characteristics, behavior, lifestyle, and natural environment of the python and the anaconda.
  1. Reticulated python—Juvenile literature. 2. Anaconda—Juvenile literature. 3. Reptiles—Juvenile literature. [1. Pythons. 2. Anaconda. 3. Snakes.] I. Lockwood, Judy. II. Title. III. Series.
QL666.O6F45   1988   597.96—dc19   88-5421
ISBN 0-89686-391-3

International Standard Book Number: 0-89686-391-3	**Library of Congress Catalog Card Number:** 88-5421

PHOTO CREDITS:

Cover: Tom Stack & Associates: Warren Garst
DRK Photo: (Don & Pat Valenti) 7; (Belinda Wright) 23; (Peter Pickford) 24
Tom Stack & Associates: (John Cancalosi) 4, 8, 12, 19, 30, 35;
  (Cris Crowley) 9, 11, 25; (Gary Milburn) 15; (M. Timothy O'Keefe) 16;
  (Tom Stack) 20; (David M. Dennis) 26, 28-29, 38-39, 42-43;
  (Bob McKeever) 27; (Chip Isenhart) 32; (Brian Parker) 36
Acknowledgement to Herpetologist Susan F. Schafer, San Diego Zoo.

Copyright © 1988 by Crestwood House, Macmillan Publishing Company

All rights reserved. No part of this book may be reproduced or transmitted in any form or by any means, electronic or mechanical, including photocopying, recording, or by any information storage and retrieval system, without permission in writing from the Publisher.

Macmillan Publishing Company
866 Third Avenue
New York, NY 10022
Collier Macmillan Canada, Inc.

Printed in the United States of America
First Edition
10 9 8 7 6 5 4 3 2

TABLE OF CONTENTS

Introduction: Giant snakes 5
Chapter I: The world's two largest snakes 6
    Finely-tuned senses
    Snakes on the inside
    Snakes on the outside
    How the giants move
Chapter II: Feeding habits of the giant snakes 14
    Detecting prey
    Types of prey
    Catching and constricting prey
    Swallowing the big meal
Chapter III: Old World snake—the reticulated python 20
    At home on land or sea
    Laying eggs, ignoring hatchlings
    Other large pythons
    Smaller python relatives
Chapter IV: New World snake—the giant anaconda 31
    Inhabitant of watery places
    Tracking the solitary giant
    Bearing live young
    Another anaconda
Chapter V: People and snakes 37
    Are giant snakes dangerous?
    How old? How long? How many?
    Enemies of the giant snakes
    Giants on the Threatened Species List
Map 45
Index/Glossary 46-47

The world's largest snakes live in the hottest, rainiest areas of the earth.

INTRODUCTION:

Deep in the Amazon jungle, a South American anaconda slides silently along the river bank. The huge snake slips into the slow-moving waters until only its eyes and nostrils show above the surface. The anaconda waits for prey.

On the other side of the world another giant snake lies still. Its body is almost hidden in the overgrowth of the southeast Asian jungle. Suddenly it senses the heat of warm-blooded prey. As a jackal nears, the reticulated python springs and throws its huge coils around the unsuspecting animal. The patient hunter has found its next meal.

The giant anaconda and the reticulated python are only two of the 3,000 different kinds of snakes found around the world. Only a few hundred of these snakes are poisonous. Most snakes are harmless and play an important part in keeping nature in balance by controlling the rodent population.

Snakes are legless reptiles with long, slender bodies. Other members of the reptile family are turtles, tortoises, lizards, crocodiles, and alligators. Reptiles have scales or plate-covered bodies, breathe air, and have hearts and lungs.

Snakes have been on the earth 125 million years. Scientists think snakes evolved from lizards. Snakes, like other reptiles, are cold-blooded, which means they depend on their surroundings to keep them warm. A lizard, for example, may sun on a garden path or a turtle may bask on a log to stay warm. Snakes, too, need the sun's heat to keep them warm and active. If they get too cold, they may die. Many snakes hibernate when the weather gets too cold. Their metabolism, or body activity, slows, and they sleep through the winter.

The world's biggest snakes don't hibernate. They live near the equator, in the hottest, rainiest areas of the earth. In this climate they can keep their huge bodies warm.

This book is about the world's largest snakes, the giant anaconda (*Eunectes murinus*), the reticulated python (*Python reticulatus*), and some of their relatives.

CHAPTER ONE:

Anacondas and pythons are alike in many ways. Both are members of the *Boidae* family of snakes. All pythons belong to the subfamily *Pythoniae*.

Giant anacondas and reticulated pythons are some of the longest animals of the world. They could stretch from the back seat of a school bus all the way to the dashboard!

Both are primitive snakes. Unlike many sleeker, shorter snakes, these giants have room in their big bodies for two lungs, set side by side. They both have tiny spurs near the base of their bodies. The spurs were probably legs at one time. The spurs hardly show and

At one time, the hidden, tiny spurs at the base of a snake's body were probably legs.

Anacondas do not poison their prey; they constrict an animal so it can't breathe.

don't help the snakes move at all, but males use them when courting females.

Like all giant snakes, anacondas and pythons are constrictors. They don't use poison to kill their prey. Instead, these snakes squeeze (constrict) an animal so that it can't breathe. When the animal suffocates and its heart stops beating, the snake eats the animal whole.

Anacondas and pythons are alike in many ways. They're long and big with heads and bodies of similar shape. Both snakes are good swimmers and will hunt

Because they do not have eyelids, a clear cap protects the snakes' eyes.

for food in water as well as on land.

Finely-tuned senses

Snakes have no eyelids and therefore cannot blink. Instead, a clear protective cap covers each eye. Like a window, this eye covering is part of the snake's skin. The clear eye scale protects the eye and keeps it from drying out. The eye scales also let snakes see underwater, just like goggles help a diver.

Even though snakes have no outer ears, they do have a sense of hearing. Vibrations pass through bones in their heads to tiny bones in their inner ears. Scientists think these vibrations help snakes sense when prey is near, or warn them of danger.

The snake's forked tongue is not a stinger. The tongue helps the snake smell. When the snake's tongue flicks out, it picks up scents from the ground and air. When the tongue ficks back in, the smell passes into the Jacobson's Organ in the roof of the mouth. The nerves in this special organ react to the smell and send signals to the snake's brain.

Snakes on the inside

The giant snake's backbone runs the length of its body. Humans have only 33 or 34 vertebrae in their backbones, but snakes may have up to 400 vertebrae! Flexible joints between the vertebrae make it easy for snakes to twist. Strong ball and socket joints lock the snake's vertebrae together. One vertebra fits into the next, much like a baseball fits into a firmly held baseball glove. This is a perfect design for animals that bend and squeeze. These joints make the snake flexible. Strong muscles attached to the snake's skin cover these bones.

Snakes can twist in many directions because of flexible joints between the vertebrae.

A snake's scales form many interesting and unique patterns.

A pair of curved ribs are connected by muscle to the scales of the belly. Since the ribs are not anchored to any other bone, the snake can easily expand its body to swallow a big meal.

Human's intestines are bunched up inside their bodies. No room for that in a snake. There is just one loop inside the snake's small intestine. Snakes have a canal, like a long flexible tube, from throat to vent (the opening between the body and tail where waste is expelled).

Snakes on the outside

Overlapping scales are part of the outer layer of the snake's skin. They cover the snake in a one-piece, water-resistant tube. When these big snakes are at rest, their inside curves may have big wrinkles, while the outside curves are tight and smooth.

Like folded-over skin, the snake's overlapping scales make it easy for the snake to eat a big meal. The skin on its belly is one row of thick, large scales. These scales can expand like an accordion. The scales on the snake's back are smaller and more complex than the belly scales. These smaller scales often form beautiful designs, like patterns worked with tiny tiles.

A snake's skin is flexible, but it doesn't grow with the snake. Beneath each layer of skin, a new layer forms. Several times a year the snake sheds its top layer, usually in one piece. The snake rubs against the ground or rocks to help remove the old skin. The giant snakes are especially beautiful right after shedding, when their colors are brightest.

How the giants move

The reticulated python and the anaconda use their belly scales like mini-tractor treads for traveling. One muscle on the snake's belly pulls the scales forward and another pulls the scales backward. With this rectilinear motion, the back of the scale catches the ground and the snake pushes against it. Bit by bit the snake inches forward. The snake can move fast, but only for short distances. For these larger snakes, getting around is slow business.

CHAPTER TWO:

Big snakes don't eat three square meals a day. In fact, four huge meals a year may be enough for these giant snakes. Warm-blooded animals burn up food energy much faster than the giant snakes. Anacondas and pythons can go many days or weeks without eating, but they usually eat more often than that.

The giant snakes can be big eaters. A 25-foot (7.6-meter) python once ate two goats in one day and an antelope a few days later. That's 138 pounds (62 kilograms) of food in less than one week!

Detecting prey

Humans have developed infra-red sensing machines which pick up body warmth and project red images of people or animals on viewing screens.

Pythons, anacondas, and some other snakes have

"Pits" are located along a python's upper jaw.

built-in infra-red sensors located in "pits" on their faces. Pit vipers, like rattlesnakes, have just one pit. Pythons and boa constrictors have a row of pits along their upper jaws. In pythons the pits are in each of their scales. The pits have nerves which sense heat changes. The nerves send an image of warm-blooded prey to the snakes' brains, much like the infra-red sensing machines humans use.

The giant snakes often hunt at night. Their facial pits help locate prey. By moving their heads back and forth, the snakes can find prey even on moonless nights.

Measuring an anaconda is a tricky job!

Types of prey

The anaconda is one of the world's most powerful constrictors. Living in swamps or on the banks of slow-moving rivers, the anaconda eats land animals as big and ferocious as the alligator-like caiman (pronounced KA-mun), which can be six feet (1.8 m) long. The anaconda also eats turtles, fish, birds, and small mammals. The python's prey includes lizards, birds, antelopes, monkeys, jackals, sheep, goats, and chickens.

Most snakes' prey weighs less than 50 pounds (22.5 kg), but the world's largest snakes can eat a 100-pound (45-kg) meal. That's like eating 400 quarter-pound hamburgers for lunch!

Catching and constricting prey

All of the largest snakes are constrictors. With their strong jaws, sharp teeth, and powerful bodies, the anaconda and python are well-designed for catching prey.

A python waits on a riverbank in Burma, a country in southeast Asia. It senses nearby prey. When a wild pig moves closer to the water to drink, the giant snake lunges suddenly, grabbing the unsuspecting pig with its needle-sharp teeth.

At the same time, the snake coils its huge body around the animal and squeezes tighter and tighter. When the pig lets out air to take a breath, the snake squeezes harder. Unable to breathe, the pig soon dies.

Swallowing the big meal

Now the snake begins a difficult job—getting the food into its stomach. Since the snake's jaws are not made for chewing, it must swallow all of its meals whole.

The snake's jaw is an engineering wonder. Human chins are made of bone connected to bone. A person's mouth can only open as wide as these rigid bones allow. In snakes, a tough band, called a ligament, joins the right and left halves of the bottom jaw together at the chin. Like a sturdy rubber band, this ligament lets the snake's jaw stretch apart. The jaw can spread wide open for swallowing big prey like the wild pig. At the back, the bottom jaw also comes apart from the upper jaw, so the snake's mouth can get even bigger. With these double-hinged jaws and a flexible throat, the snake can swallow prey much larger than its own head.

Bit by bit, the snake gets the prey into its wide open jaws. The snake's thin, pointed teeth curve back. Like spiked entryways to parking lots which let cars go in only one direction, the teeth only let the food go into the snake. Abundant saliva in the mouth and throat helps the food slide in.

The pig slides through the snake's mouth and into its body. The snake's stretchy skin now does its job. The skin folds of the python make the snake almost elastic. The python can expand to make room for the whole pig. The python's ribs also spread apart so the big meal will fit.

Getting the prey past the throat may take more than an hour. The snake's windpipe extends along the

A rat makes a tasty meal for this python.

bottom of its mouth like a straw. The snake can breathe even while swallowing prey.

Until the food is digested, it shows as a big lump in the snake's body. Days may go by before the prey is digested. All that's left when digestion is complete are bristles, feathers, and claws. The python expels these as waste through its vent.

CHAPTER THREE:

"Reticulated" means "covered with a network." The python's scales form a beautiful design, or network, of rich browns, golds, and blacks. Reddish eyes and a black line from the snout to the back of its head make it look different from other pythons.

A reticulated python named Colossus lived at the Highland Park Zoo in Pittsburgh, Pennsylvania, for 30 years. It measured 28.5 feet (8.5 m) and weighed 300 pounds (135 kg). Usually, pythons only grow to about 20 feet (6 m).

Reticulated pythons like living near water.

At home on land or sea

Reticulated pythons live in the "Old World," the hottest, wettest parts of southeast Asia, the East Indies, and the Philippines. Pythons like being near water and have flourished in big cities. In the past, pythons found it easy to live along the riverbanks of cities like Bangkok, Thailand. They hid in crevices during the day and found plenty to eat at night. The giant snakes stowed away on cargo ships, often surprising people who opened packing crates when the ship landed. Zoos often got their pythons by capturing these trapped pythons!

Like most pythons, the reticulated python is a good swimmer and has even been found in the open sea. In 1888, a great volcano on Krakatoa Island in southern Indonesia erupted, killing all living things. After the eruption, a reticulated python was one of the first reptiles to reach the island. It probably swam from the island of Sumatra or Java—many, many miles away!

Laying eggs, ignoring hatchlings

Pythons are oviparous (pronounced o-VIP-uh-rus); they lay eggs from which the young hatch. Even though pythons pay no attention to their young, a female python takes unusual care of her eggs.

About a month after mating, the python lays up to 100 eggs. They're not brittle like chicken eggs. All of the eggs have tough, flexible coverings. The female python pushes the eggs into a high pile, then coils her long body around the stack, resting her head on top.

Amazingly, the python incubates the eggs, raising its body temperature up to 12 degrees above its normal temperature. The python's eggs thrive in this warmth. For the next 80 days, the python only leaves the eggs to find a drink of water. The rest of the time she warms and protects the eggs.

When the young are ready to hatch, the mother snake glides away. The hatchlings are on their own. An egg tooth, a sharp tooth that protrudes from the hatchlings' upper jaws, helps the tiny snakes slit open their leathery shells. This egg tooth falls off soon after the young snakes have escaped their shells.

The hatchlings look like miniatures of their parents, but they are only 2 to 2.5 feet (0.6 to 0.8 m) long. They catch and constrict small prey for food with no lessons at all.

Other large pythons

The giant reticulated python has many relatives. The Indian python is big and beautiful. Its bold

Grasslands and watery lowlands are the favorite habitat of the Indian rock python.

pattern is a mix of light and dark browns. This python has pointed markings like arrowheads on its head. The Indian python, found in India, Ceylon, and the East Indies, reaches a maximum of 20 feet (6 m) in length. These pythons make their home in grasslands or watery lowlands. The Indian python swims well and can hold its breath underwater as long as 30 minutes.

The Indian python's prehensile (gripping) tail makes tree climbing easy. Hanging down from a limb by its strong tail, the Indian python can strike at

The African rock python can grow to 25 feet!

nearby prey. Although it's not common, Indian pythons have been known to eat leopards or impalas (African antelopes).

The African rock python is the third largest giant snake. It can reach 25 feet (7.5 m) in length, but is usually 13 to 20 feet (5 to 6 m) long. Its colors are a deep coffee brown on a light brown background with specks along the sides. It's the only giant snake in Africa. The rock python can live in many places—forests, farming areas, mountains, lakes, swamps, and small rivers. The only place the African python can't live is the desert.

The amethystine (pronounced am-uh-THIS-tun) python, named for the purple mineral amethyst, has purple markings on its yellow-brown skin. Most amethystines grow to 10 or 15 feet (3 to 4.5 m). They live in Australia, New Guinea (a country north of Australia), and many of the Pacific islands. The amethystine is more slender than the other giant snakes. While some people say the snakes eat kangaroos, most amethystine pythons are satisfied with smaller animals like chickens.

The fierce-looking amethystine python has purple markings on its skin.

The smaller Calabar ground python lives underground.

Smaller python relatives

The burrowing or Calabar ground python lives below the ground. Three feet (0.9 m) long, its tube-like body and blunt head are perfect for underground life in west and central Africa. When crawling on land, it keeps its short tail up. Stories about two-headed snakes might have started with this snake.

The royal python or ball python of west Africa

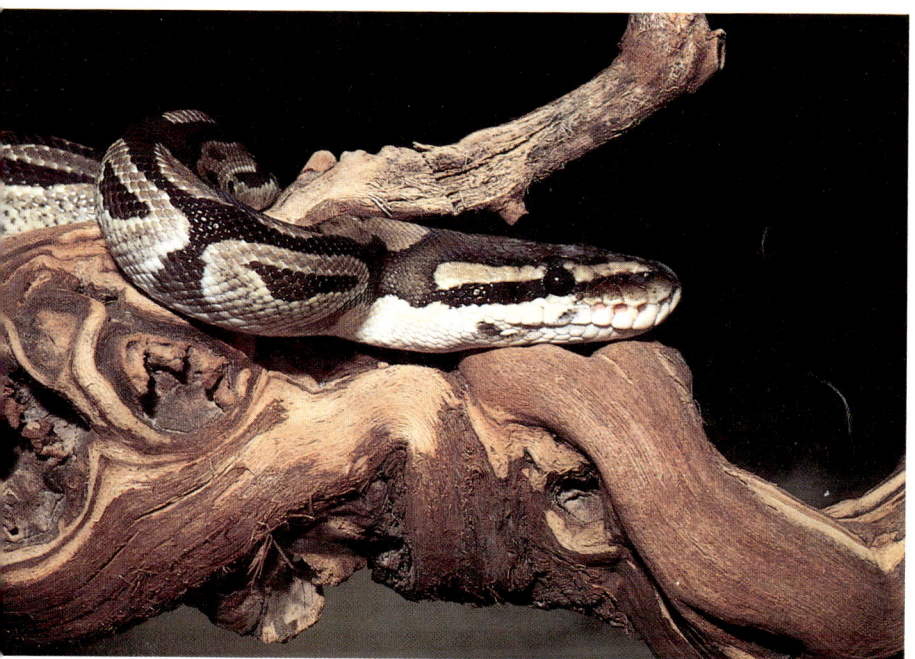

When it is in danger, the royal python of west Africa rolls into a tight ball.

reaches four to five feet (1.2 to 1.5 m) in length. To defend itself, it rolls into a tight ball with its head in the center. When it is coiled this way, the snake can be rolled around like a ball.

The seven-foot (2.1-m) green tree python is well-adapted to its leafy environment. It's at home among the green, leafy branches in New Guinea. With its prehensile tail, the green tree python can perch high in trees and strike at birds flying by! The emerald tree boa is a look-alike cousin. Their resting positions are the same. Like thick rope, they loop their bodies over

Most people will only encounter giant snakes at the zoo.

The green tree python loops itself over a branch and hangs its head in the center of its coils.

a branch, leaving their heads in the center of their coils. Coiled this way on a branch, the two snakes are hard to tell apart.

The Australian python, found in trees, on the ground, and in the waters of New Guinea and Australia, is a fine rodent catcher. It's often used to control the rat and mouse population in grain storage areas.

CHAPTER FOUR:

The reticulated python will never meet the giant anaconda. The anaconda lives only in the "New World," the steamy tropics and jungles of South America's Amazon and Orinoco Rivers, an area almost as big as the United States.

In the bright, wet rain forests, far from cities and people, the jungles teem with life. The air is filled with sounds, and bright wings flash under a leafy umbrella of huge trees. Stunning flowers and vines shelter bees, sloths, howler monkeys, anteaters, frogs, and toucans.

Inhabitant of watery places

The anaconda spends its time in or near the water. This muddy-green tropical giant is found on the

The Australian python is often used as a reliable rodent-catcher.

banks of lakes, in the slow-moving river waters, or in swamps.

Unlike the python, the anaconda has no design formed with its scales. Instead, the anaconda has true spots. These big round circles of black against drab olive green skin, and blotches of orange outlined with black on its sides, make good camouflage. The snake's eyes are mounted quite high on its head, so the snake can be on the lookout when resting in the water. A black line runs from its eyes down to the broader sides of its skull. The snake's scales are glossy and smooth.

The anaconda is truly a giant among snakes. The reticulated python may be longer, but the anaconda weighs more. A 17-foot (5.1-m) anaconda might weigh as much as a 24-foot (7.3-m) python!

A 20-foot (6-m) anaconda weighs as much as a hefty 250-pound (112-kg) football player. A full-grown anaconda could weigh 330 pounds (148 kg).

Compared with other snakes, the anaconda is not slender. This stocky snake may measure three feet (0.9 m) around its middle. That's as big around as a sports car's steering wheel.

For its combination of great length and weight, the anaconda gets the prize for being the world's biggest snake. Anacondas, also called water boas, can grow to 29 feet (8.8 m), which is much longer than any other South American snake.

Tracking the solitary giant

Observing the giant anaconda is not easy. In the wild, this snake lives in a vast area of land and water. It may return to sleep in one place out of habit, but even that changes. The Amazon rain forest is far from civilization. It's expensive and difficult to study one anaconda over a long period of time. The snake makes no sound except an occasional "hiss" and leaves no trail.

Anacondas are loners. They don't live in any kind of family group. Studying leopards, a herd of buffalo, or even birds is much easier than studying anacondas.

Leopards can wear a transmitter on a collar, and birds can get a lightweight band on their legs. But there's no place to attach a tag to a giant snake. If herpetologists (people who study reptiles) can get the snake to swallow a small beeper, they can track the snake for several days. But, eventually, the beeper will pass out of the snake's body as waste.

The anaconda usually does his silent hunting at night, adding another challenge to a scientist. Imagine trying to follow a giant anaconda around its watery habitat in the dark!

Studying anacondas in captivity probably doesn't give a complete picture of what they're like in the tropics. While many snakes adapt well to captivity, the anaconda is nervous, jumpy, and prone to biting keepers with its long teeth. Many mysteries remain about this large snake.

Bearing live young

Like other boas, the anaconda is ovoviviparous (pronounced o-vo-vie-VIP-uh-rus). This means the eggs stay in the snake until they hatch, then the snake

Scientists have had a hard time studying the silent anaconda.

bears live young. Based on what is known about other boas, mating probably takes place sometime in the spring when a male and female anaconda find each other by scent. They intertwine to pass the male's sperm to the female's eggs.

Herpetologists are not sure how many young are born at one time. Probably two to three dozen tiny anacondas are born in August or September. Like python young, anacondas are on their own from the beginning. The adult does not train or protect them.

Another anaconda

The giant anaconda has a South American relative, the yellow or Paraguayan anaconda. Even less is known about the yellow anaconda than the giant anaconda.

The much smaller yellow anaconda lives farther south in South America. This snake grows to about 15 feet (4.5 m). When young, the yellow anaconda is a distinctive yellow with black markings. These markings fade as the snake matures.

When young, the Paraguayan anaconda's scales are yellow with black markings.

CHAPTER FIVE:

Humans aren't automatically afraid of snakes. When young children are introduced to snakes in positive ways, they're interested in these remarkable reptiles.

Many people are surprised to find that snakes are not slimy to touch. They feel dry and will be cool or warm depending on their surroundings.

People are curious about the back-and-forth "S" movement of the smaller snakes, the varied patterns and bright colors of many snakes' scales, and the great differences in size, looks, and habits.

Are giant snakes dangerous?

Few people will ever meet giant snakes like the anaconda and the reticulated python face to face. If travelers in Asia or the Amazon do come upon a giant snake, they are in little danger. Generally, an anaconda will slide beneath the surface of the water rather than confront people.

While the anaconda and python are very strong, several adults together can escape from them with a

Some people think that a snake's skin is slimy, but it usually feels dry.

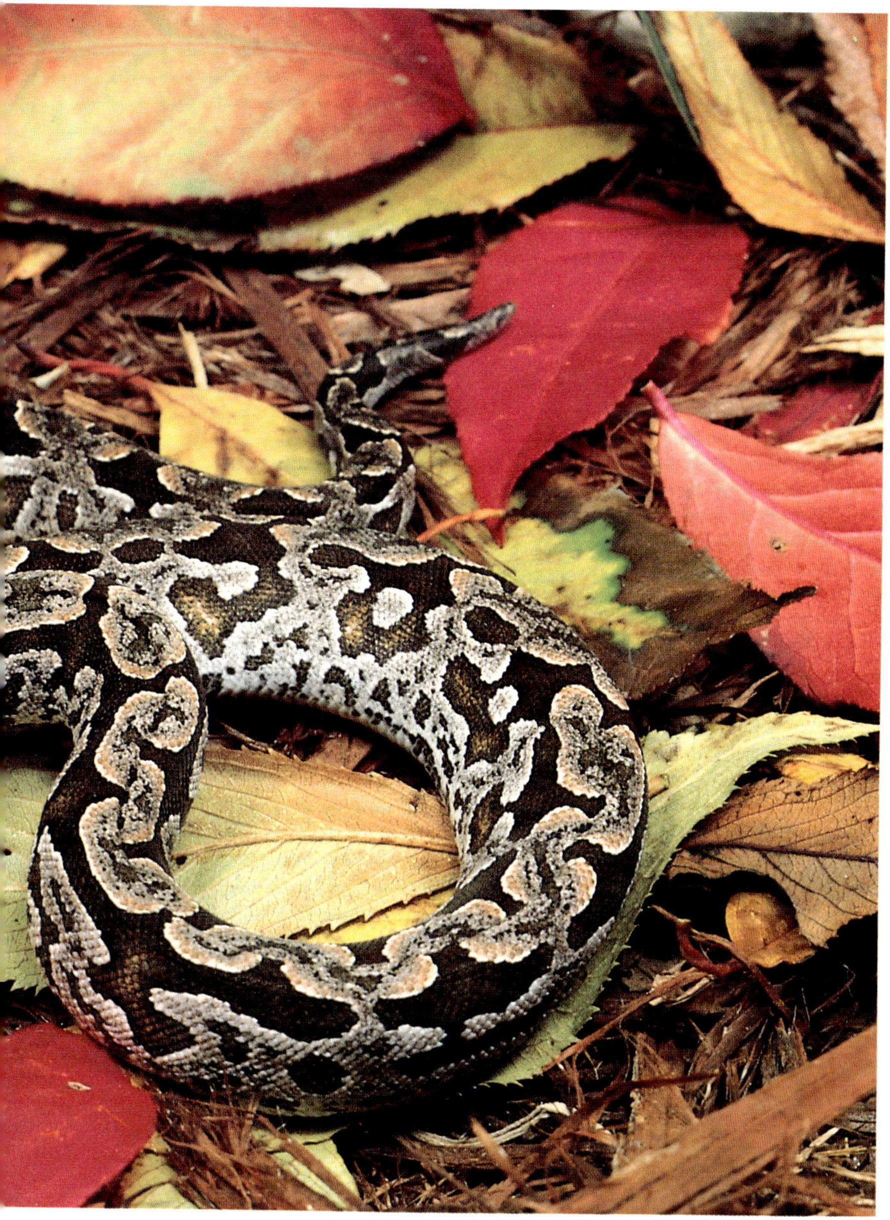

struggle. There have been a few cases when large snakes have surprised a person who's alone. They have wounded, killed, and even eaten a small person. Usually, reports of anacondas and pythons attacking and eating humans are not true.

How old? How long? How many?

Nobody knows for sure just how long the giant snakes can live. Zoo records show a 20- to 30-year life span for giant snakes. But in zoos, snakes face no dangers. They receive good care and excellent food. It's hard to know if snakes in the wild live that long.

Like the fishing stories of "the one that got away," stories about the length of giant snakes are greatly exaggerated. No one has ever shown proof of 60-foot (18-m) or 80-foot (24-m) snakes.

Measuring a giant snake is difficult. The usual way is to run a string along the length of the snake from tip to tail, then measure the string. But even that is tricky. The problem is the snake's overlapping scales. If several snake handlers move a live snake, it can be stretched out longer than normal. This happens even more when the snake is dead. And when just the skin is measured, it may be many feet longer than the snake was because all the overlapping folds are smoothed out!

People disagree on the size of the giant snakes. Some say the biggest pythons are close to 30 feet (9.1 m); others say 33 feet (10 m). The exact numbers don't matter. Scientists do agree that the reticulated python and the anaconda are the world's longest snakes. Today, pythons and anacondas often measure 20 to 25 feet (6 to 7 m).

No one knows how many giant snakes exist today. They live in such vast and largely uninhabited land areas that counting them is impossible.

Enemies of the giant snakes

When young, the baby reticulated python and anaconda may be prey for bigger animals. But with every foot the snakes grow, their enemies decrease. Few animals could take on the giant snakes and come out alive. Some people say a troop of baboons or a herd of wild pigs could attack and possibly kill a giant snake. But it would be a rough fight. The animals would face deep bites from the snake's needle-sharp teeth as well as the danger of constriction.

All snakes, including the python and anaconda, are on the Threatened Species List.

43

Giants on the Threatened Species List

The biggest threat to the giant snakes is humans. As the world population grows, more and more areas of the world are being used for housing and farming. That makes less room for the anacondas and pythons.

Every snake in the Boidae family, the giant anaconda and the reticulated python included, is on the Threatened Species List. That's just one level below endangered, meaning close to extinction. Some snakes have already been listed as endangered species.

The giant anaconda and the reticulated python are fascinating animals. They live in mysterious, faraway countries. Most of the time they keep to themselves and don't deserve their scary reputation. Herpetologists will continue to study and learn more about the giant snakes' habitats and life styles.

There's a chance that as humans use more and more of the world's land, varieties of these splendid giant snakes that haven't even been identified may vanish.

MAP:

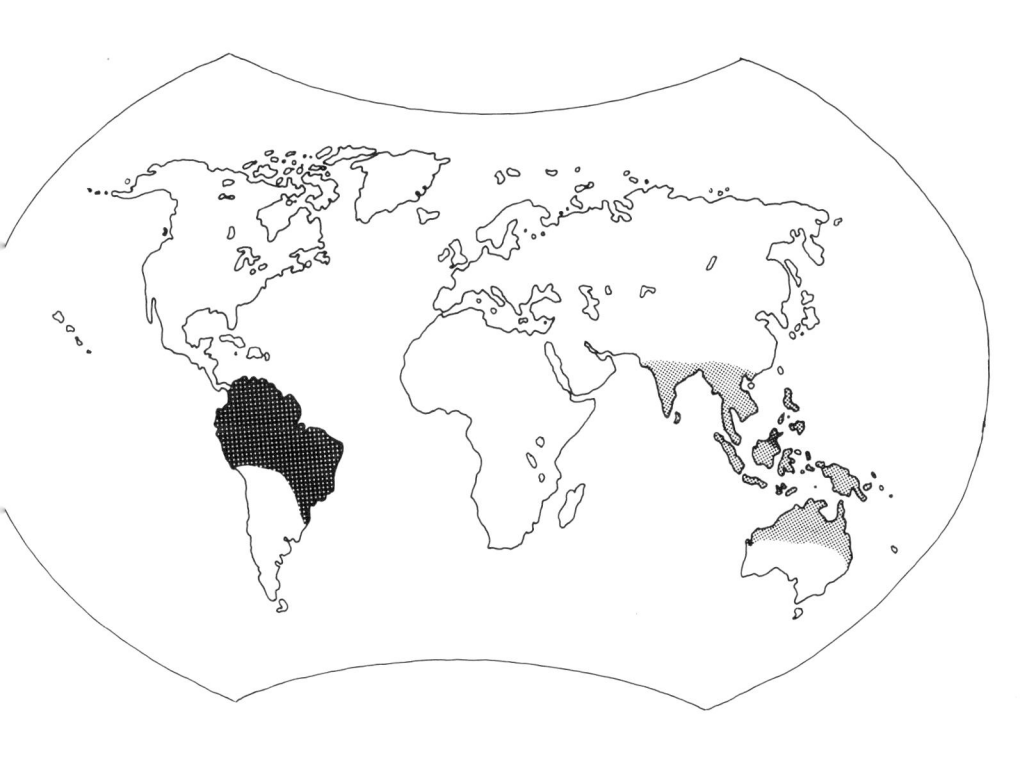

▓▓▓ **Most anacondas live within these areas.**

░░░ **Most reticulated pythons live within these areas.**

45

INDEX/GLOSSARY:

BOIDS 6, 44—*Snakes belonging to the family Boidae, including boas (anacondas and boas) and pythons.*

COLD BLOODED 5—*An animal having a body temperature that changes according to the temperature of the surroundings.*

CONSTRICTORS 8, 16, 17, 22, 41—*Snakes which kill their prey by wrapping tightly around the animal and squeezing. The prey is unable to breathe and suffocates.*

EGG TOOTH 22—*A sharp tooth on the head of young reptiles used to help snakes escape their leathery shells. The egg tooth falls off after hatching.*

EXTINCT 44—*The loss of an animal, as when the last member of a species dies.*

EYE SCALE 9—*A clear cap that covers and protects a snake's eyes. The eye scale is part of a snake's skin.*

HATCHLINGS 22—*Young reptiles which hatch from eggs.*

HERPETOLOGIST 34, 35, 44—*A scientist who studies reptiles and amphibians.*

HIBERNATE 6—*To spend the winter in an inactive sleep-like state.*

INCUBATE 22—*To warm eggs by the heat of the sun or the female's body.*

JACOBSON'S ORGAN 10—*The organ in the roof of a snake's mouth that helps snakes smell.*

LIGAMENT 18—*A band of tough tissue that connects bones or cartilage.*

OVIPAROUS 21—*An egg-laying animal.*

OVOVIVIPAROUS 34—*An animal that produces eggs that hatch within a female's body. The young emerge live from the mother's body.*

PIT ORGANS 15—*Heat sensors located on or between the scales of a giant snake's mouth.*

PREHENSILE 23, 27—*Adapted to grasping, holding, or wrapping around something, as a snake's tail.*

REPTILES 5, 21, 34, 37—*A class of cold-blooded animals with a backbone and lungs. Reptiles usually have skin covered with horny plates or scales.*

INDEX/GLOSSARY:

RETICULATED 5, 6, 13, 20, 21, 22, 31, 33, 37, 41, 44— *Covered with a network; refers to the reticulated python's complex scale design.*

RETICULATED MOTION 14—*Moving straight forward by pushing on the ground with the scales on the belly.*

VENT 12, 19—*An opening between a snake's body and tail through which waste is passed.*

VERTEBRAE 10—*The bones connected together to form a backbone or spinal column.*

WILDLIFE
HABITS & HABITAT

READ AND ENJOY THE SERIES:

If you would like to know more about all kinds of wildlife, you should take a look at the other books in this series.

You'll find books on bald eagles and other birds. Books on alligators and other reptiles. There are books about deer and other big-game animals. And there are books about sharks and other creatures that live in the ocean.

In all of the books you will learn that life in the wild is not easy. But you will also learn what people can do to help wildlife survive. So read on!